How Bodies Work

Claire Llewellyn

W

FRANKLIN WATTS

LONDON • SYDNEY

First published in 2005 by Franklin Watts
96 Leonard Street, London EC2A 4XD

Franklin Watts Australia
Level 17/207 Kent Street, Sydney NSW 2000

Text copyright © Claire Llewellyn 2005
Design and concept © Franklin Watts 2005

Series adviser: Gill Matthews, non-fiction literacy
    consultant and Inset trainer
Series editor: Rachel Cooke
Editor: Sarah Ridley
Series design: Peter Scoulding
Designer: Jemima Lumley
Illustrations: Ian Thompson
Photography: Steve Shott, unless otherwise credited
Acknowledgements: Graham Bool Photography 16; Chris Fairclough title page, 19l; Jim
Cummins/Corbis cover, 21; Peter Millard 5r; Ray Moller 4l, 5l, 9t, 12r, 13l, 14, 20, 22l, 23; Gunter
Ziesler/Still Pictures 5br.

Thanks to our models: Charlie, Eliza, Estelle, Joe, Kayne, Mariela, Osman and the Kwan family.
Thanks also to Mrs Tarpey and St John's Green School for their help with the photography.

A CIP catalogue record for this book is available from the British Library.

ISBN: 0 7496 6365 0

Dewey decimal classification number: 612

Printed in China

Contents

Our bodies

We all have a body.
Our bodies can do
many different things.

► *Our bodies
can walk.*

▲ *Our bodies
can eat.*

▶ *Our bodies can shout out loud.*

▼ *Or they can sit, quietly reading.*

Can you
wriggle like
a snake?

The parts of the body

Our bodies have many parts. Some of them are on the inside.

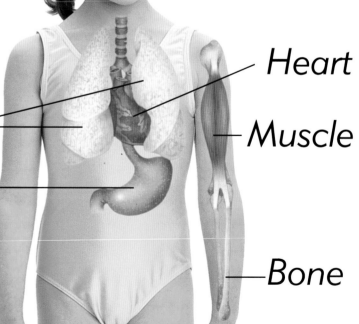

Lungs

Stomach

Heart

Muscle

Bone

▶ *Here are a few of the body parts on the inside.*

Other parts are on the outside.

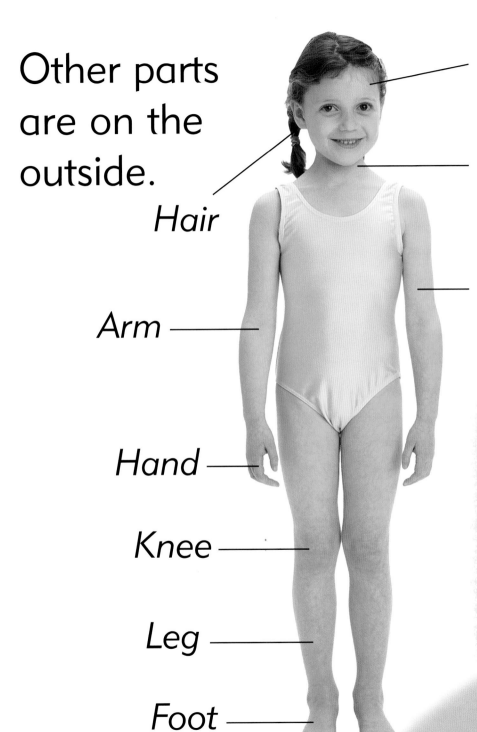

Head

Neck

Hair

Skin

Arm

Hand

Knee

Leg

Foot

Animals have many body parts, too. Can you name some animals that have wings, fins, tusks or hooves?

7

Our skin

We have skin all over our body. It helps to keep out germs and dirt.

▲ *Skin comes in different colours.*

▲ *Skin is waterproof.*

When we cut our skin, a scab grows. This helps the skin to heal.

▶ *The Sun can harm our skin. Protect it with suncream and stay in the shade at midday.*

How the body moves

We have bones and muscles inside our body. They help us to move.

▶ *This boy's muscles are pulling on bones as he plays the violin.*

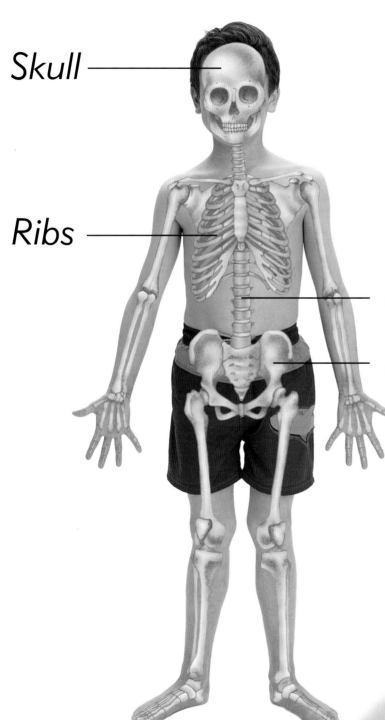

Skull

Ribs

Backbone

Pelvis

◀ *Our bodies are held up by a bony skeleton.*

Can you feel bones inside your body? Where?

The senses

We have five senses.
These are seeing, hearing,
tasting, smelling and touching.

▼ *We can see with
our eyes…*

▲ *hear with
our ears…*

▼*smell and taste things with our nose and tongue...*

Our senses send messages to our brain. They tell it what is happening around us. How does this help to keep us safe?

▶ *and touch things with our skin.*

Food for the body

Food gives us energy and helps us to grow.

◀ *We need to eat food and drink water to stay alive.*

Our food moves from one end of the body to the other!

1. We chew the food.

2. *It is mashed inside our stomach.*

3. *Food moves along a tube. The goodness in the food passes into our body.*

4. *Waste leaves our body when we go to the toilet.*

How do you feel when you have eaten a meal?

15

Oxygen for life

When we breathe, we take in air. The air contains a gas called oxygen. We need it to stay alive.

◀ *We breathe harder when we exercise.*

► We use our lungs to breathe. As they fill with air, our chest gets bigger.

Windpipe

Lungs

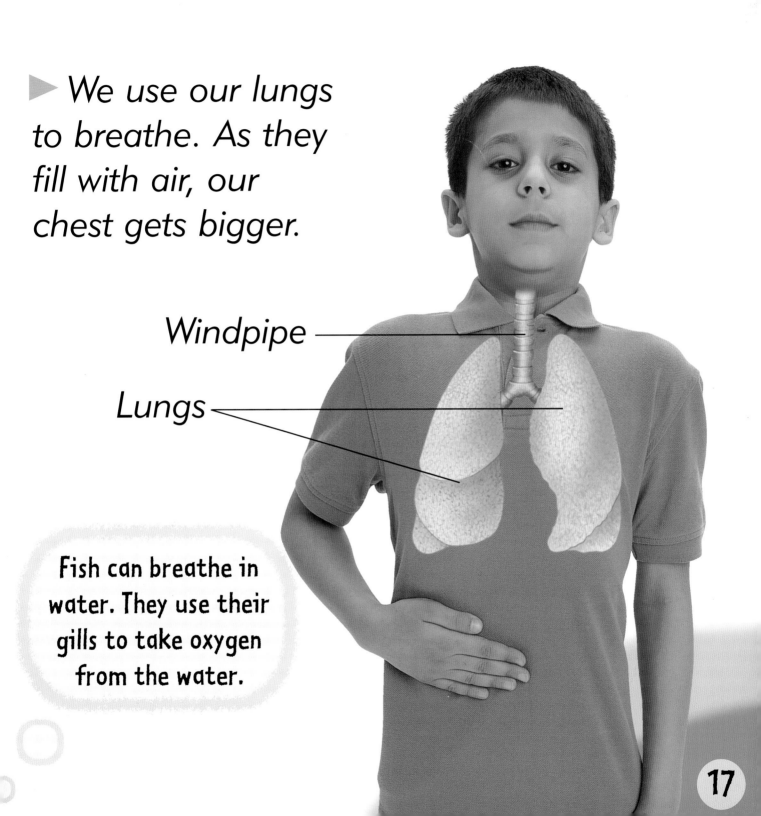

Fish can breathe in water. They use their gills to take oxygen from the water.

Blood in the body

Blood flows around the body in blood vessels. They carry food and oxygen to every part.

▶ *The blood is pumped around by a muscle called the heart.*

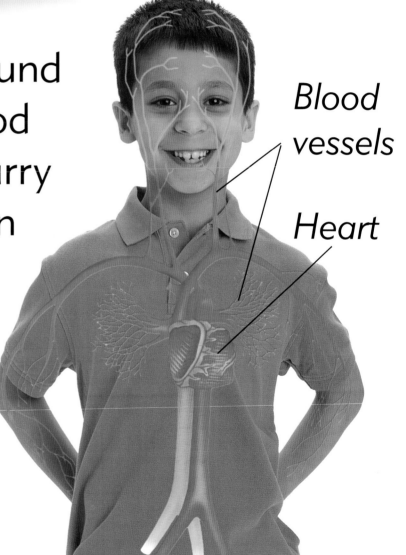

Blood vessels

Heart

▼ When we exercise, the heart pushes the blood around faster.

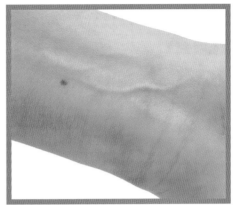

▲ In some places, we can see the blood vessels under the skin.

Do you ever feel your heart beating? When?

Time to rest

All day our bodies work hard.
At night they need to rest.

▶*While we are growing up, we need a lot of sleep.*

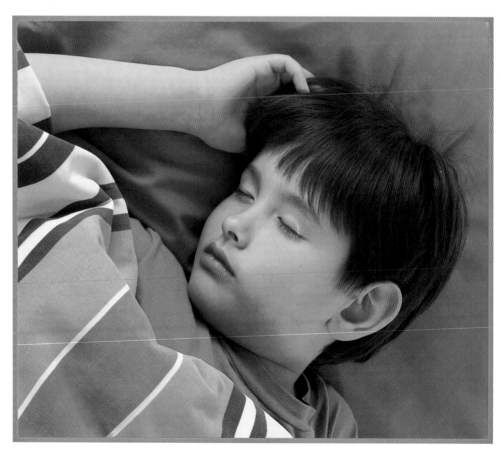

▼ *Sleep gives us energy for the day ahead.*

How do you feel when you have had a bad night's sleep?

I know that...

1 Our bodies can do many things.

2 The body is made up of different parts.

3 Our skin keeps out germs and dirt.

4 Our bones and muscles help us to move.

5 Our five senses help us to understand the world.

6 We need to eat and drink to stay alive.

7 We also need to breathe oxygen.

8 The heart pumps blood around the body.

9 At night our bodies need to sleep.

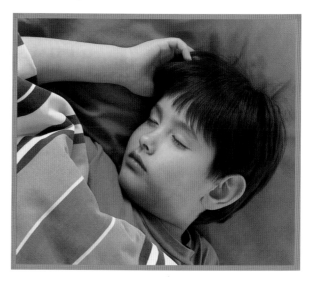

Index

About this book

I Know That! is designed to introduce children to the process of gathering information and using reference books, one of the key skills needed to begin more formal learning at school. For this reason, each book's structure reflects the information books children will use later in their learning career – with key information in the main text and additional facts and ideas in the captions. The panels give an opportunity for further activities, ideas or discussions. The contents page and index are helpful reference guides.

The language is carefully chosen to be accessible to children just beginning to read. Illustrations support the text but also give information in their own right; active consideration and discussion of images is another key referencing skill. The main aim of the series is to build confidence – showing children how much they already know and giving them the ability to gather new information for themselves. With this in mind, the *I know that...* section at the end of the book is a simple way for children to revisit what they already know as well as what they have learnt from reading the book.